There Are Some So Unlucky
They Don't Even Have Bodies

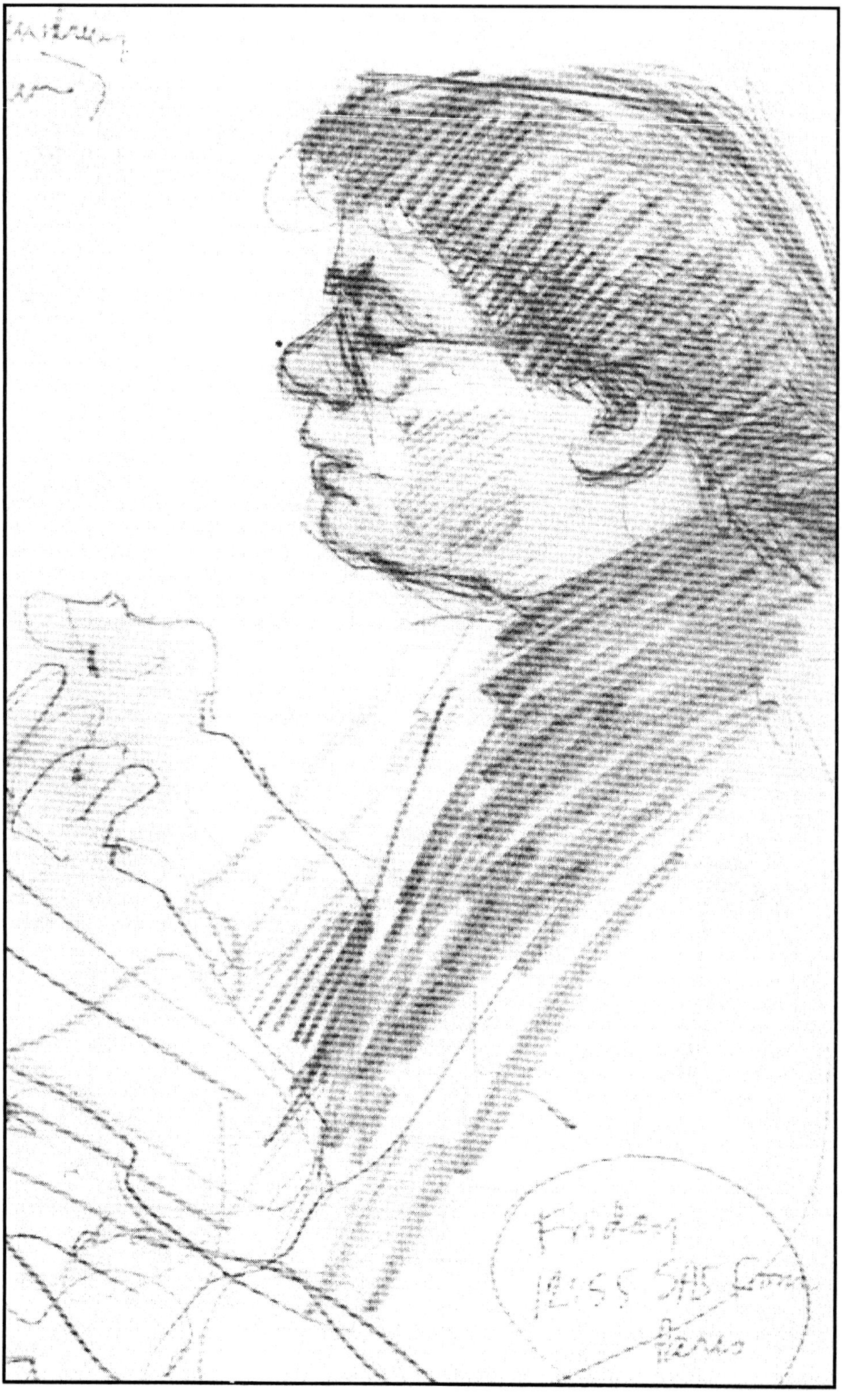

There Are Some So Unlucky
They Don't Even Have Bodies!

Richard Olafson

Ekstasis Editions

National Library of Canada Cataloguing in Publication Data

Olafson, Richard
 There are some so unlucky they don't even have bodies!

Poems.
ISBN 1-894800-18-4

I. Title.
PS8579.L23T43 2003   C811'.54   C2003-910747-4
PR9199.3.O383T43 2003

© Richard Olafson, 2003
Cover Art: Hildegard von Bingen
Frontispiece: Heather Spears, in Paris

Published in 2003 by:
Ekstasis Editions Canada Ltd.   Ekstasis Editions
Box 8474, Main Postal Outlet   Box 571
Victoria, B.C. V8W 3S1   Banff, Alberta T0L 0C0

The Canada Council | Le Conseil des Arts
For the Arts | du Canada
Since 1957 | Depuis 1957

British Columbia Arts Council
Supported by the Province of British Columbia

There Are Some So Unlucky They Don't Even Have Bodies! has been published with the assistance of grants from the Canada Council and the Cultural Services Branch of British Columbia.

To Carol and Devin and Jeffrey

*For the soul outwears the body,
As the sword outwears its sheath...*
            Byron

The selfyeast of the spirit a dull dough sours...
            Hopkins

CONTENTS

Please Come In	11
Riddle	12
Finding a Name	13
Two Branches on the Tree of Being: Heraclitus or Pythagoras?	14
For the Winter Dead	15
Elegy: A Poem for Luella	16
Four Songs Before Birth	19
Planting Placenta by Moonlight	24
Naming the Baby: A Poem for My Son	26
Learning to Walk	27
Praise	29
Joy and Sorrow	31
A Blessing	32
Wings of Ash	33
Untitled 1	34
Untitled 2	35
Death Evens	36
Praise Being	37
Moments of Pure Being	38
The Name of Being	40
Bookmarks	42
Traids: For Autumn	43
Wordshadows	
Sun	44
Moon	48
Stars	51
Poem for Spaceflight	53
Song of Nothing	54
Beneath the Many Stars	55
Ovid's Void	56
An Island in the Light	57
End of Day: Evening	58
The Sea Between Two Islands	59

Becoming	60
Star Flesh	61
Coho Ferry Farewell	62
Little Song for Autumn	63
Ezra Cranko	64
Radar	65
A Song of Resurrection	72

Please Come In

*Until you turn this page
You will not know me.
Until now you have not
Come in.
To enter, turn the page.*

*Until now your have not
Been a guest in this
House of words.
Accept my invitation
To come in.*

*Please come in
And be a guest
Dine at the soul's table.
Please come in.
Please turn the page.*

Riddle

Between life and death
There is something else.
What is it?

Finding a Name

A name sculpts.
The meaning in being.
Or the being in meaning.
Stone. Sculpted by naming.
Marble. Name sculpture.
Geologist. Layers of shale.
A fossil.

Two Branches on the Tree of Being: Heraclitus or Pythagoras?

Heraclitus saw reality
A shattered crystal glass.
All roots are fire, the being-tree
Consumed by it; nothing lasts.

Pythagoras discovered tonality
A blacksmith's anvil in the sun
Struck out all harmony; the being-tree
Nourished by music. All is one.

For the Winter Dead

The trees bough down
Humble to the wind.
October is winding about
The roots of all beings.
The air is fragile like glass
If you breathe you
Might break it.

The wind blows leaves
Away and the winter dead
Awaken; a dim light
Will not despair the blood.
Sap freezes the veins,
Leaves, so brittle with frost,
Might break on the breath.

All nature redeems the body
In death and sap flows into
The blood. Earth retrieves
The body from winter ground,
Stars do not oppose the heart:
The body is so brittle
If it breathes it might break.

Elegy: A Poem for Luella

I

A black crow in your eyes flying
between the boughs of your temples,
the last time I saw you alive in hospital
you were dying on an autumn day
potent with rain, though the sun still shone.
We spoke of your book, your final eloquence,
and the long-stemmed roses I brought to your bedside.
A gentle sleep rocked your body
to rest, as the soul moves through darkness
into light. I did not know then
your were dying. I promise not to mourn
for the body but to praise the soul.
Time passes within the body:
passes and the soul chimes at midnight
for time within the body has ended;
the flesh is a clock that surrounds us.
The world unravels, the strings that
bind us are tangled. Your brow is furrowed
in the shape of a bird in flight, flying
beyond the shore towards the light.
Gull or crow? Which is your soul?
Do not mourn. Do not mourn.
Souls unite with flesh again and we
that are left within the world must
go down now into the well of grief
and drink there the waters of pain and joy.
I have made for you a book, what is left
of the body is nothing but words, and
memories of you dying in November, the month
when trees let go of their leaves.

II

Go down to the lake of grief.
Speaking over your grave, I felt
the tug of being towards that light,
your body in ashes. I thought clocks would
stop and an alarm would sound out.
When you died I wanted to ring the chimes
of time, bells ring out in the tundra
of the heart. There was only silence, deep silence
like the vision of a lone gull flying over
the lake of grief in autumn.
Go down and drink the water of grief;
go to where the body and spirit are one,
two rivers meet on desolate rocks.
The spirit is the only body!
In life we hover between being and nonbeing
so long that when death finally comes
we complete ourselves, and the world
persists in grief and splendour.
Death gives a kind of lucid birdness
to your melancholy wings.
The still life you gave us, with your signature
in the corner, remains over our living-room couch:
a lamp with Victorian shade, a table, a bracelet,
your abstract of a butterfly, the lamp's shadow,
the light. Your body in the earth, your mind
in the air, your spirit swimming salmon-like
in water, your poems, burning embers of being.
Over you gulls and crows rise above the
waters of sadness, sculpt the gravestone clouds.
The silence of poetry surrounds you, the word
created as one makes bread, gives us now
a final poem. A death in autumn
the season when flowers let fall their petals.

III

Go down to the sea. Wave upon wave
has come to this shore of the body.
Many autumns have come and gone
in the body, many waves crash against
this shore. This flower dying lays
bare its stem in the centre of being.
Words alone cannot express the dark,
the deep dark of silence. My wife and I
keep each other company after the funeral,
when the children are in bed. Shadows outside
our window are the imagined world, the roots
and branches of poetry, scraping the pane of glass
the siding of the house of the mind, silence of poetry.
The next day we go down to the sea.
We go down in late afternoon when the tide
of night ascends the shore of language.
We go down now to where two waters converge
and the ocean of being refuses neither.
Gulls and crows at war beyond the shore, wings beating
like waves curling, rasping cries in anger and conflict.
Gulls and crows within the world swing out
from land, and sing, a scratch across the stillness,
sing joyful praise in autumn sun, for all the light there is.

Four Songs Before Birth

       I

Your belly, your belly,
Double being
Two natures
Of one woman.
Thou.

II

The leaves have all fallen
From the pear tree in our backyard.
You undress in darkness
Surrounding us,
Light shining off your belly.

The moon casts shadows
Below your breasts, a tide
Rising in small light from your belly
A bare pear tree, the moon,
This night, your belly, before bed.

III

Your belly swells
With the moon: tidal swell.
Ocean of being.

A child grows in light
With your body: the day.
Garden of hearts.

In the shadow of the moon
Your belly: another shadow.
Seam of light.

Come out of light, comes
This child into shore:
Boat of love.

Your body full of light
Afloat within: casting shadows.
Cloud of knowing.

Your belly, a boat,
Tidal flow: our hearts.
Wave of being.

IV

I love your nightime
Nakedness,
Love

Your belly
Round
Beneath the covers

A small fist
Pokes my ribs

The baby
Unborn
Floats
Towards us.

Our two natures

Floating
In
Air.

Our child
Moves
To make room:

A wave shimmers
Across
Your belly

Your belly
Warm to my fingers
Burns with being.

Your body
Full
Below the sheets.

Planting Placenta by Moonlight

All year long, a heart grew
in the loosely turned soil
of our backyard: the garden, after winter
rained on, grown wild with weeds.
After midnight, under the chill light
of stars, scattered seeds fertile
in the sky, the sparks of love
lit up within us. Our backs
to the house, a small child sleeps in his cradle
recently born, unnamed yet,
the name of being unsayable yet.
He is not disturbed by the rap
of the spade tapping the ground
to find a soft place to plant
the placenta, one month after
his birth, near the hour of his birth.

Light breaks in shadows, a wave
at the edge of our garden: the moon
balances on the cedar fence.
I take the spade to the farthest edge
of the garden and cut
through the loose topsoil. My wife holds
the placenta, rich with blood
in a plastic jar. A stone dug up
in the packed clay and the buried potatoes
scattered loosely there, like lost stones.

We went out after midnight
to plant in our garden a seed
nurtured in our bodies for nine months.
The stars so close to us, a taste
on our tongues, the coarse soil
caressed by our hands, at the back garden
where the birthcord of morning glories are
tangled in strawberries.
In the heart-shaped placenta
the roots of a tree whose branches entwine.
A raw bone of blood, the ribbed blood vessels
bulge with the tree of life. A seed of light.

A stone planted in our garden nurtured
this just-born child in liquid sleep.
The garden bruised by the spade's rough entrance
parting the earth's lips, the tongue's unshaped
language of being, a mouth open
to say the unsayable, silence we cannot speak.
This was the seed house in which this tree
was shaped, the world garden, a womb opens
to receive again a grain.
Beyond the light of our home, where only
the moon and stars illuminate our ritual
for next autumn's harvest
we plant this small acorn of being.

Naming the Baby: A Poem for My Son

Around your cradle we circle
Your namelessness, and seek to prune

A name from the highest branch
Or our family tree, all our family

One body still lit up
Within by the mystery of birth.

A first smile on your still fresh face, I shine
Above the changetable in the bedroom

And a diaper comes off, diaper rash on your skin,
Smarts, a fern in a fossil: a child's cry is a dark

Geology of the heart. Your fingers grasp my hair
With tiny hand still emergent from the water's

Source and swim salmon-bred
Towards a genealogical sea.

A name charts the geography of soul
Casting a net into the flowing river

Of consciousness. A forest hides you,
A game we play with our palms

And with my hands I massage
Your feet to calm you

And on the light-spattered branches I poke aside
The tang of spring on the leaves releases a resonance

On the tongue, stuttering your name in my praise
Charges my breath with hard vowels, gentle consonants.

Learning to Walk

Learning to crawl, this small child pulls his body
backwards, into the room. My wife and I act
as coaches as he learns the sport of moving.
The world moves under him as he takes
his next movement with tiny palms
and holds the floor. When he stands, a chair
for balance, he is like some young animal
green with life, a body in spring bud.

I have been walking now for thirty-seven years
and this tiny boy is just beginning to take
his first tentative steps. The art of walking
is a moving into the consciousness of pain.
As the years go by my feet have cut a path
through the world that leaves a furrow
on my brow. Watching him, we cringe with each
fall. With each failure he screams, crying
for us to take his pain away. Should we provide him
with a map that he may avoid grief?

One who knows grief is most near the heart,
said to me, "The body is a burden and a blessing,
but the spirit is contained in the body as cargo
in a boat." The body carries its own weight and by walking
one learns to carry the body's weight
through life. One of the many gifts of the body
is movement. By walking, colliding and falling
with every object in our house, you will learn the body's
weight and the grief of failure,
the joy of success, when your step is sure.

This morning when you left the bed in wet diaper,
waking me to help you put on your brother's
hand-me-down cowboy boots, you shine with pride.
Now no longer a swaddled babe,
no longer mobile only by our cuddling arms,
steady feet have given you a new status
a toddler at last toddling through mischief.

At our bedside you pose smiling prankishly
in your new costume, and waddle awkwardly
into the next room. May you by walking
know the earth turning under your feet on grief,
a long spiral down history, and by standing
tall, though less than three feet high
in your small body, know exultant joy.
The floor is yours, my son, you were born
to stand upright and walk as a fish
is born to swim in water.
The floor is yours. It is hard
when you fall and will cause you pain.
But it is yours. Take it
one step at a time.

Praise

Praise all things ephemeral.
Everything that exists moves,
Changes, becomes another.
The breath enters and leaves
The body, a moment becomes
Another moment, a shadow
Becomes another shadow.
A cloud moving across the sky
Opens the world to light,
Night becomes day, day leaves
The world in darkness.
This waterfall cascading down
A mountain slope wears down
Stone, running to one source.

Praise transformation, the pulse
And pull of being. The moon
Moves through its cycles full,
New moon, crescent and full.
Seasons rotate about the centre
Of existence, while moments slide
Through us; the dim gloom of winter
Flows into green spring. Moments
Gathered like a harvest, a river
Of change flows by. Birds, insects
The marmot's hiding, the wilderness deer,
You and I become one through
Transformation, all unified, all in flux between
Being and nonbeing, presence and absence,
Appearance and essence, all visible
In change.

Praise death for it is not
The end of things. All are
Changed by it, consumed by the fire
Of death. Night moves towards the light.
Living and dying, negative and positive,
All become one through death.

Praise all the light there is
Left, the moon over the ridge,
The sun going down, the morning
Just beyond the night, pulsing
With being, all verges on
Night, all blessed by change.
Daylight will always come again.
Let us now praise all ephemera,
For nothing remains
In the glory
Of change.

Joy and Sorrow

Fragile and ephemeral is this joy, grief
could break it. My garden in the morning
grown over with weeds, reading in the light.
Sunlight through leaves, pears are falling
and rotting on the ground.
Of joy I know these few things:
my children's passionate play, the playground
of life, the hiding in the tall, uncut grass.
My children swinging below the trees and
I permit myself to swing with them.
For grief I substitute joy.

Sorrow is exhumed by joy.
Sorrow rises in the sun tide of light
with joy. Sorrow and joy
Eternal twins. Shadow
of my shadow in the light
of morning, reading
the book of grief.
We are all salmon swimming to die.
Joy is here and now, this moment,
the moment's peace!

A Blessing

Stepping darkly through
The night's rain
In confusion, I do not know
Whether to exult or despair.
Looking up, the moon's afterlight
Tells me the rain
Does not matter
Everything is quiet, expressing nothing:
Life is a great blessing!

Walking after midnight
I stumble, a little drunk
with many moods, I do not know
Whether to choose joy or grief.
A little too drunk for that.
The moon never changes
After midnight.
Calm, and central to all that is:
Life is a great blessing!

Walking in the morning, night
Lifting from my eyes, spring light
Awakens the earth below with the roots
Of flowers to come. The sun
Brings perfect clarity;
Neither happy nor sad,
I do not choose between joy or despair,
Pain or respite from pain, wind or sun.
Flower, stone, tree and sun
Fish and fowl, mammal and reptile
All become one in the scope of glory,
All that exists knows
Life is a great blessing.
Life is a great blessing!

Wings of Ash

An eagle soars out from the high cliff
Of thought—a lifted gesture

Rising from the heart of the earth.

A white seagull passes by, redeemed by flight
A hand moving across the sky into light.

A cupped mind riding a sea of wind.

Alone in the moment, a solitary word
Surrounded by silence, you become that bird

And earth retreats beneath your feet.

Your flight towards absence a kind of seam
That divides the world from dream

You are not diminished by but smoothed into flight.

You are pulled from this earth flapping
Your wings into the sun, the eagle's wings of ash floating

Into light, burning feathers to cinders

The thought's predator falls amidst the flames
The eagle pierced by the lonely ferns:

The ground comes too close to him, the white bird escapes

His loose beak, and rides the morning mist now
Wings beating towards absence and becoming.

Untitled 1

Every day I get ready to die.
A black crow cawing
Outside my bedroom window
Calls me as I wake.

Untitled 2

If the world is forest
The dying of the body is
Leaves falling, wind blowing.

A moment to bless,
This ground, this sky, a leaf
Upturned, the wind blows away.

DEATH EVENS

Death evens.
Even death
will take us all
into a great white hall.
No breath leave us
in the long slope
above a level land:
death will bevel
all beings.
No voice give us
speech. The end leave us
silent and waiting.
Death:
the line that splits
above from below.
Straight place to come to
when we bring all that is new
and make it old.
Death is cold.
We will live till we break
sleep till we wake
draw air till our breath
leave us.
Our lives smooth as smoke;
we will love till darkness
take us
and nothing is left
not
even death.
Death evens!

Praise Being
for Charles Brookman

Praise the sun for it has come to give us
Warmth: your visionary eye flies in the light
Like the wind. The light is gathered like clouds
In our hands that reach and grab the sky.

Praise the stars for they startle
The night: there would be darkness
Without them. The light of their
Shining makes me wonder at the light in us.

Praise the sky for it covers our head:
The clouds scoop up the wind and hollow
The sky beyond our seeing. The sky
Is illuminated by all the light there is!

Praise each day that we may see the next:
I waken to the light shining in all beings,
A warm bath, filled with praise for the body.
At night, there is praise left for the next day.

Praise all beings in that morning light!

Praise being. Praise being.

Moments of Pure Being

I.

The trees grow from stone
as my body grows from life.
There are moments like this
when days are full of pure being.
The earth is quiet in the soul
and the soul steps out of the body,
detached from the spinning centre
of self. Naked, stepping into a forest
that is all one. The self joins
the earth, as a man joins
a woman in love, as flesh joins the soil
in death. But the body is never dead
although it sleeps. The body rises up and walks
through all the world's moments
when everything is at rest but utterly sensate.
A stillness like a leaf falls
upon the self, and everything in the body
goes quiet to absorb the silence.
Then suddenly a small bird goes twittering
still clinging to the moment,
like the body to soul, like the wind
that blows the leaves away.

II.

Late at night
I hear the unending beat
of rain upon my roof and the earth
soaking it in. The wet earth
breaking at night
like a woman beside me. The evening
turning green with the growing life
of the forest. The expanding sky
a container, a clear belljar,
for the energy moving out
from the soaked land. The rain
joins the sky to the earth, a link
between the air above and the core
at the centre beneath me. The soil absorbs,
like a sponge, the nourishment of the rain.
The rain nourishes the earth
as women nourish men. The pure moments
are those that pass between us,
when something is given. Rain falls
from the sky like something given.
I hear it moving over me
inside the shell of a dry but damp house,
a strong bond of love
between two universal elements.

The Name of Being

Suppose the world ended one day?
What would be left of the wind?
The sea would have no shore
to come to, the sky
no place to send the light.
The clouds sing
in a void, and the rose's nipple
blossom no more
in the garden of the world's heart.
Suppose the world ended one day
and all it left behind was Being?

I wanted a name
but without a world
there is no poet.
I want to write my name
but there is no pen
without a world.

I am more like an absence
than a thing, more like a colour
than a shape.
I am the air and not the wind.
The hummingbird's dive
will find no nectar
in a void without that petal's shape.
Life is wind that comes and goes.
A man who watches the waves
is living more than ever the sea.

The seagull's flight. The dawn.
The sun and moon joined at night.
Grass. Trees. Flowers.
All gone, all gone away.
Being is a light that turns on and off.

Suppose the world lay down in weariness
and no longer wanted to Be?
Would there be a greater possibility
of Being than ever before?
Everything in the world
is made of light. Birds
that fly backwards,
mountains that avalanche
on lovers, voice in a void.
All is colour and shape,
things and absences, vacuum
and fullness, all gathers,
a cluster at Being.

I could be the wind, a diamond
rusted by carbon.
I could be a swallow
and fly backwards
into a mountain's cavernous mouth.
The thunder would be my voice
and the lightening my eyes.
But suppose?
Suppose the world went away one day
and had no place to go to?

Bookmarks

Late September.
Blackberries are sour,
take heart.

*

What are the sounds
the mind makes?

*

In the heart's garden
a flower of words
blossoms.

Triads: For Autumn

Stars shine out in the night—
Constellations slide down a slope
of sky to the sea.

A lightness of body.
Everything that lives healed
By flowing water.

Winter frost on leaves.
Chilled breath, air begins to freeze.
Robins stop their song.

Wordshadows

I. Sun

*

Delight in the world's light.

*

Hands gather sheaths of light.

*

The day begins again: light!

*

All flows upward: plum tree.

*

Light fades into the leaves.

*

The sky consumed by light.

*

Hand hesitates above a flower.

*

The rose of noon glows.

*

Flowers of light: hollow stems.

*

Daylight centred between two nights.

*

Flowers of words blossom: silence.

*

Morning sun shines: being. Be!

*

All flows downward: waterfall breaks.

*

The heart aches for light.

*

Light shines through the mist.

*

Praise the new day begun!

II. Moon

*

The moon unfurls a pearl.

*

Among trees: a deep dark.

*

Angels undrape an iceberg cloud.

*

I wake drunk with moonlight.

*

A bird sings in darkness.

*

In the shadow: another shadow.

*

A moon overwhelmed by tides.

*

The moon will fall soon.

*

Moon ascending tides of light.

*

Deep silence of the ocean.

*

Sleep, O World, lie still!

*

A flight of birds: death.

*

Come, take the dark away!

*

Bless the light of night.

III. Stars

*

The night eroded by stars.

*

We are all stars underneath.

*

Stars are within our bodies.

*

Sparks of love in night.

*

Stars revolve within and without.

*

Each breath is a death.

*

Those born are already old.

*

Moon within moon, stars within.

*

Eternity of stars, perpetual light!

Poem for Spaceflight

Let us now find
A way to the centre.
The garden, after summer,
Is grown over with weeds.

The soil rich with life, the earth
revolves around a sun: stars
In darkness: a light!
The path outward
Leads us to the centre.

Song of Nothing

Out of nothing we are born and
      to nothing will we return.
The morning dark moves in an ocean of night.
Wake from winter's sleep. Rise up
      like a lion in the light.
Out of nothing we are born and to
      nothing we will return.

Learn the lessons of death
      from the evening star.
Above and below, far and near,
      have no perspective.
Listen to what death has to say:
This is one moment.
Out of nothing we are born and
      to nothing we will return.
Out of nothing we are born and
      to nothing we will return.

Beneath the Many Stars

The moon stalls in
An elliptical orbit.
The wonder of wonder below the sky.
The stars are out another night
And the shining seeks the firmament.

Stars beneath the feet
Where I walk on the various grass.
A drop of dew reflects the light of the stars
And the wind, the music of the night.

    Stars.
        Moon.
            Night.

Ovid's Void

The most fatal disease of this consumer-driven world
is boredom! What kills the spirit most is boredom.
Dirty dishes in the sink and laundry to be done.
Tristia, tristia, omnia tristia,
I look into the mirror each morning and it's me again!

Harsh fruit of the quotidian earth
another sun follows another sun
and we button and unbutton our shirts going
to bed and then waking up, breakfast waits
while slicing and dicing onions
Ovid said the most difficult, the most painful thing about exile
was boredom, and today I feel exiled from the ordinary.
O Te Deum, Te Deum, God of boredom, comfort me!

One afternoon spent lying beside a lake of stars
I have committed the unspeakable sin of an active life.
O Te Deum, forgive me for being sometimes interested in life
and even occasionally being interesting when
friends do not quickly turn their backs when I speak.
If there was one thing that killed Giordano Bruno it was
being extraordinary in an ordinary world.

The wonder of each moment shudders through me like a spark
Ennui, ennui, my friend, my lover, I embrace you in the dark.

An Island in the Light

Because of this, I could not tell
What my dreams foretold. Night centred

Like an island in the light. The shadows
In the woods. The breeze twisted

In the funnel of the bay. The cliffs folded
Into the sea. Gulls skimming

Over the water in the bright noon.
The sky lit up at night with the red

Glare of the sun going down. The still
Water drifting with light shining

Out in the morning rainbows
Climbing the clustered stone grown over

With moss above the sea on the island
In the centre of the light of my body.

END OF DAY: EVENING

Sing for what light there is
Left: The sun going down is
Blessed. Morning will
Come again.

The Sea Between Two Islands

Primal waves lulled
Into the rocking of the wind,
Calmed by the cleavage
Of the sheltering breasts
Of two islands shaped
In a funnel of brine.
Waves curl against
The shore among the stones
Of an isolate sea.

Sunshine on the surface
With light shining out
Water broken by
The skimming of the gulls.
Wings beating
In staccato drafts
The wind gathered
Sonorous in a solitary wave.

Becoming

Each day I start over.
The beginning moves me
to an end. Each day
I kill the man I am
to make a new child in me.
I give birth to morning
and wake to a new self.

I enter the day reluctant
to know from where I came.
I am not a moment, but a process
of moments. I remember a beginning
like the pure sky unfolded,
but I stand between sky and earth,
always becoming, always waking
to a new day, neither begun nor ended.

Star Flesh

In the forests of the night
Our bodies are leaves falling, broken
Boughs, flesh roots, sap pulsing.

In the waters of the night
Our bodies are waves, shore eroding
Waves crashing against island bones.

In the pastures of the night
Our flesh is grass, wind whipping
Flesh dust, stars sparking over grass.

In the forests of the night.
In the waters of the night.
In the pastures of the night.

Forest flesh, night water, grass stars:
O night, our bodies are sparks, casting off
Flesh, making stars, the world's light.

Coho Ferry Farewell

Morning light pulls us over the strait
mist above the water, the outline

of Port Angeles in the distance.
Another shore widens to let a

stranger in. August, even in bright summer
has chill seawinds that stretch from shore to shore.

There is a moment when leaving
when farewells mean so little.

A moment while leaving when there is no goodbye,
a thousand farewells have brought me to this emptiness.

Little Song for Autumn

Late September. Blackberries are sour, take heart
For night is cooler and it is time to live
Again. The eye grabs a falling leaf
By its colour, a woodpecker chops at the forest,
And night fills the lungs, take heart.

September is ending and the trees recede
Into sleep. Flowers are falling and the clouds
Weep at night. Let the cold fill your heart,
Night sings from the wood's lungs.
Autumn has come, winter will soon appear, a barren
Breath is in the air. I am alive
Once more, take heart.

Ezra Cranko

Proud old Ez, in the Pisan Pound
An old dog, caught in the meat
Of dead civilization! A loud
Vocalbus, full of stuttering force and heat.

Radar

*

morning

*

soil

*

breath

*

ground

*

ember

*

stone

*

ooze

*

tongue

*

love

*

muscle

*

mirror

*

stride

*

meat

*

open

*

afterlight

*

flux

*

rose

*

body

*

surge

*

death

*

ocean

*

flight

*

miracle

*

desire

*

silence

*

blossom

*

pearl

*

seed

*

forest

*

star

*

consume

*

rain

*

eye

*

wind

*

flow

*

wave

*

absence

*

alone

*

bird

*

shadows

*

lace

*

roots

*

endure

A Song of Resurrection

There are some so unlucky they don't even have bodies.
A cloud blown by wind—this body of pain
Would cast no shadow under a blinding sun,
Would light up the deadened dark of night.
So put on your body, leave death behind.
There is no god like a god in the brain.

You say pain is bodiless: consciousness is to suffer
A pain larger than the body. The reality of pain
Is double pain and the reality of love is double love
And death, life more real that life, is twice birth.
So put on your body, leave death behind.
There is a god alive, there is a god in your eyes.

The day is going to come when life will mean
Nothing: the day will foam up like clouds
Radiating with bodiless spirits in light
Shining through: somewhere there is a world without sun.
Put on your body and die before you die:
There is no god like a god in your eyes.

Between life and absence, the cradle and the tomb
The body is, living and dying, sleeping and waking
There is the body and we are in the centre of it.
Land and sky are flesh held to flesh, and stars,
The sparks of love, are men and women making light.
There are some so unlucky they don't even have bodies.

Your body is like a flight, like a flight of stones
Dancing upon a still lake, your soul is aware of that.
A light from the stars pierces this white cloud, so wake up!
And put on your body, leave death behind.
There is no god like a god in the brain.
There are some so unlucky they don't even have bodies!